J.S. Bach
Adaptations

Piano Transcriptions by Walter Rummel

Published in Great Britain by Chester Music Limited

Head Office:

Chester Music Limited
14/15 Berners Street, London W1T 3LJ, UK.
Telephone: +44 (0)20 7612 7400
Fax: +44 (0)20 7612 7545

Sales & Hire:

Hal Leonard Europe Limited
Distribution Centre Newmarket Road,
Bury St Edmunds, Suffolk IP33 3YB

© 2009 Chester Music Limited

CH74866
ISBN 978-1-84772-893-7

e-mail: music@musicsales.co.uk
www.chesternovello.com

All Rights Reserved.

For all works contained herein: Unauthorized copying, arranging, adapting,
recording, Internet posting, public performance, or other distribution of the music in this publication
is an infringement of copyright. Infringers are liable under the law.

Printed in EU.

www.halleonard.com

Chester Music

J. S. BACH
Adaptations

PIANO TRANSCRIPTIONS BY WALTER RUMMEL

BORN in Berlin to a diversely creative family, Walter Rummel (1887–1953) was surrounded by artistic creativity from an early age. He came from a pedigree of distinguished musicians, his family home a favoured meeting place for musicians and artists. His great grandfather, Christian Rummel (1787–1849), was director of the court orchestra at Wiesbaden for Duke Wilhelm of Nassau and his maternal grandfather, Samuel Morse (1791–1892), the American painter and inventor of the telegraph.

Walter received his early musical education from his father, the noted concert pianist, London-born Franz Rummel (1853–1901), who had received professional audiences with both Franz Liszt (1811–1886) and Anton Rubenstein (1829–1894). Following his premature death, Walter's mother, Cornelia (Leila) moved the family to her native USA where piano studies continued with Samuel Fabian, himself a former pupil of Franz Liszt. During this time, Rummel became an American citizen but the cultural lure of Europe was strong and he returned to Berlin in 1904, studying piano with Leopold Godowsky (1870–1938), and composition with Hugo Kaun (1863–1932), before launching his professional career with a highly fêted double debut as pianist and composer in 1908. Following a move to Paris in 1909, Rummel soon became a close acquaintance of Claude Debussy (1862–1918), who accepted him into his inner circle of friends, and Rummel subsequently gave the first performances of twelve works by the distinguished composer, including the well known *La Fille aux cheveux de lin* and *Ondine*. Reviewers consistently praised his performances, and referred to him as a Debussy interpreter to whom 'nothing but the highest praise is due'.

The music of J. S. Bach, however, was central to Rummel's life as a creative artist, although it is likely that this was enhanced through a friendship with Ferruccio Busoni (1866–1924), whose corpus of published J. S. Bach transcriptions for piano he knew well. Encouraged by Busoni, Rummel began playing his own transcriptions, or 'adaptations' and 'Übertragungen' as he preferred to call them, and these began to appear on concert programmes as early as 1916. He would often couple his own adaptations with transcriptions by Busoni and performed them to considerable critical acclaim. A review in *The Spectator* from 1922 pronounced: 'When Mr Rummel plays Bach, neither his technique nor his personality obtrude, he so completely identifies with the spirit of the composer that we are conscious of nothing but a dazzling clarity; it is no exaggeration to say that we are *en rapport* with the musical idea in Bach's mind before it took its lifeless form in printer's ink'.

This collection of Rummel's Bach 'adaptations' for the piano draws a cross-section of twelve titles from the original twenty-five such published in a series of four publications by J & W Chester between 1922 and 1938. Belonging to a younger generation of pianist composers including Ignacy Friedman (1882–1948) and Samuil Feinberg (1890–1962), Rummel established a trend away from previous keyboard transcribers set by Liszt, Reger and others by concentrating on adapting Bach's vocal music rather than the organ works: perhaps reflecting his Calvinist faith in the titles.

The adaptations are frequently thickly scored, with bass octave doublings commonplace as evident in *Wir müssen durch viel Trübsal in das Reich Gottes eingehen*, (an early version of the D minor keyboard concerto), but this contrasts with the simplicity and effective use of the upper keyboard sonority in *Vom Himmel hoch', da komm' ich her*. In this collection, we have retained Rummel's performance directions, fingering and pedalling as originally printed. Maligned during the middle years of the twentieth century, these transcriptions are now viewed as valuable windows into historical performance practice as well as free standing works in their own right.

Like many of his contemporaries, Walter Rummel has only recently re-entered the public consciousness; a victim of the political situation in Europe of the 1930s, Rummel found himself influenced by the pro-German rhetoric of his Russian third wife. Following a series of concerts in Germany as an American citizen after the USA had entered the war, the German state refused to protect him unless he renounced his American citizenship. Forced to do this, he moved to France in 1944 as a German citizen and resumed his career before his death in 1953.

His performances as a pianist are preserved on record but this collection identifies his considerable talents as an arranger and composer — one that was especially admired by Debussy who wrote of Rummel in *The Monthly Musical Record* in 1914 that 'Among the names of the rising generation that of Walter Morse Rummel should be noted. This young musician has been matured at an early age by much culture, which has not impaired his quality of ingenious freshness; a quality so rare that one may say it is never found at the present day … Some composers are lingering over the old formulae; others overthrow everything, leaving only fugitive traces of their passage, like soap-bubbles, which, after reflecting all the colours of the prism for a moment, die away like a dream.'

James Eggleston
Chester Music, 2009.

Contents:

Dein name gleich der sonnen geh 1
Thy name, like unto the sun

Ertödt' uns durch dein' Gute! 6
Mortify us by thy grace

Ach, wie flüchtig, ach, wie nichtig ist der menschen leben 8
Ah! How ephemeral, how transitory is Man's Life!

Liebster Jesu, wir sind hier 13
Blessed Jesus, here we stand

Vater unser im Himmelreich 15
Our Father in Heaven

Was Gott tut, das ist wohlgetan 18
What God hath done, is rightly done

Stürze zu boden 24
Hurl them down headlong

Esurientes Implevit Bonis 30
(Magnificat)

Vom himmel hoch', da komm' ich her 34
From Heaven high, I come to thee

Wir eilen mit schwachen, doch emsigen schritten 36
We hasten to thee, with feeble but eager feet

Das brausen von den rauhen winden 42
The rushing of the raw winds

Wir müssen durch viel trübsal in das reich Gottes eingehen 46
Through affliction we enter the kingdom of Heaven

DEIN NAME GLEICH DER SONNEN GEH
Thy name, like unto the sun

Adapted by
WALTER RUMMEL

J.S. BACH

Note: the [ ] comprise the Aria which must be emphasised.

This collection © 2009 Chester Music Limited.

*) From this point the upper motif, subdued during the playing of the Aria, must gradually grow stronger until it overpowers the latter. From the following double bar onward, this motif is again subdued and only reasserts itself after the following 15th bar.

3

*) Here again this motif recedes, becoming prominent once more sixteen bars before the end.

ERTÖDT' UNS DURCH DEIN' GÜTE!
Mortify us by thy grace

Adapted by
WALTER RUMMEL

J.S. BACH

* 1) The tempo, which Bach rarely indicated, may in this piece lie within the limits of the two Maelzel indications.
* 2) In the original, the lower two voices are crotchets.
* 3) The last note of each chorale verse may be sustained ad libitum.

ACH, WIE FLÜCHTIG, ACH, WIE NICHTIG IST DER MENSCHEN LEBEN

Ah! how ephemeral, how transitory is Man's life!

Adapted by
WALTER RUMMEL

J.S. BACH

*) While the Chorale sounds the figuration must always remain in the background.

10

LIEBSTER JESU, WIR SIND HIER
Blessed Jesus, here we stand

Adapted by
WALTER RUMMEL

J.S. BACH

*) The upper voice must detach itself from the rest; where it dwells on quarter or half values the underlying voices must come forward thus sustaining these quarter and half values.

VATER UNSER IM HIMMELREICH
Our Father in Heaven

Adapted by
WALTER RUMMEL

J.S. BACH

WAS GOTT TUT, DAS IST WOHLGETAN
What God hath done, is rightly done

Adapted by
WALTER RUMMEL

J.S. BACH

23

STÜRZE ZU BODEN
Hurl them down headlong

Adapted by
WALTER RUMMEL

J.S. BACH

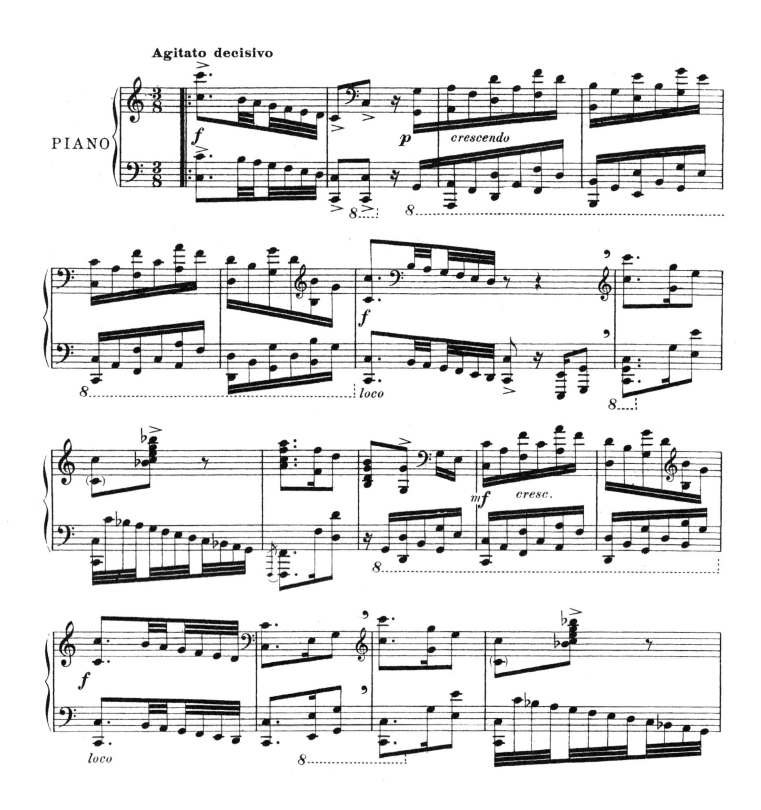

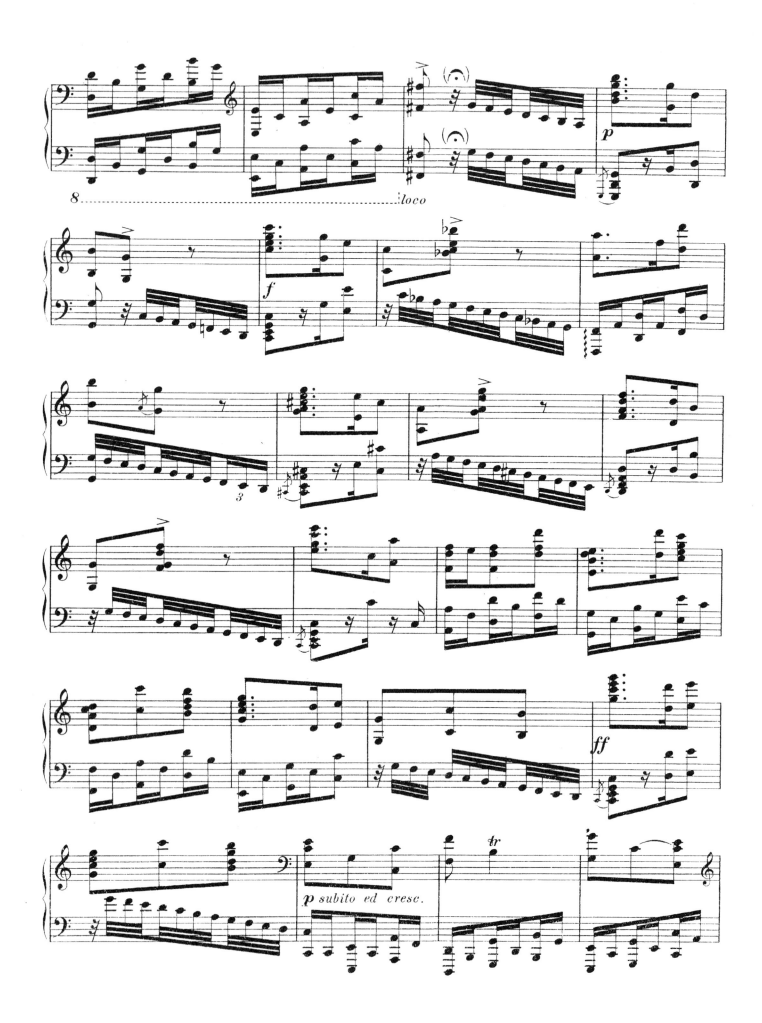

ESURIENTES IMPLEVIT BONIS
(MAGNIFICAT)

Adapted by
WALTER RUMMEL

J.S. BACH

VOM HIMMEL HOCH', DA KOMM' ICH HER
From Heaven high, I come to thee

Adapted by
WALTER RUMMEL

J.S. BACH

*) The lower octave of the Chorale should predominate here and the remaining notes are to be struck very discretly.

WIR EILEN MIT SCHWACHEN, DOCH EMSIGEN SCHRITTEN
We hasten to thee, with feeble but eager feet

Adapted by
WALTER RUMMEL

J.S. BACH

*1) In the repeat, the bars starting from here and ending *2) may be played an octave higher to give a flute-like atmosphere, while making the repetition more refreshing.

*1) The bars from *1) to *2) can be omitted in the repetition.

The bars from ★1) to ★2) can be omitted in the repetition.

DAS BRAUSEN VON DEN RAUHEN WINDEN
The rushing of the raw winds

Adapted by
WALTER RUMMEL

J.S. BACH

WIR MÜSSEN DURCH VIEL TRÜBSAL IN DAS REICH GOTTES EINGEHEN

Through affliction we enter the kingdom of Heaven

Adapted by
WALTER RUMMEL

J.S. BACH

Note: This composition must be played in strict rhythm, without the slightest variation, its whole character being destroyed unless the changeless pulsation of the beat is fully maintatined.

*) Performers who are unable to play these chords without a break may omit the upper left-hand notes in these two bars.

49

*) Performers who are unable to play these chords without a break may omit the upper left-hand notes in these two bars.

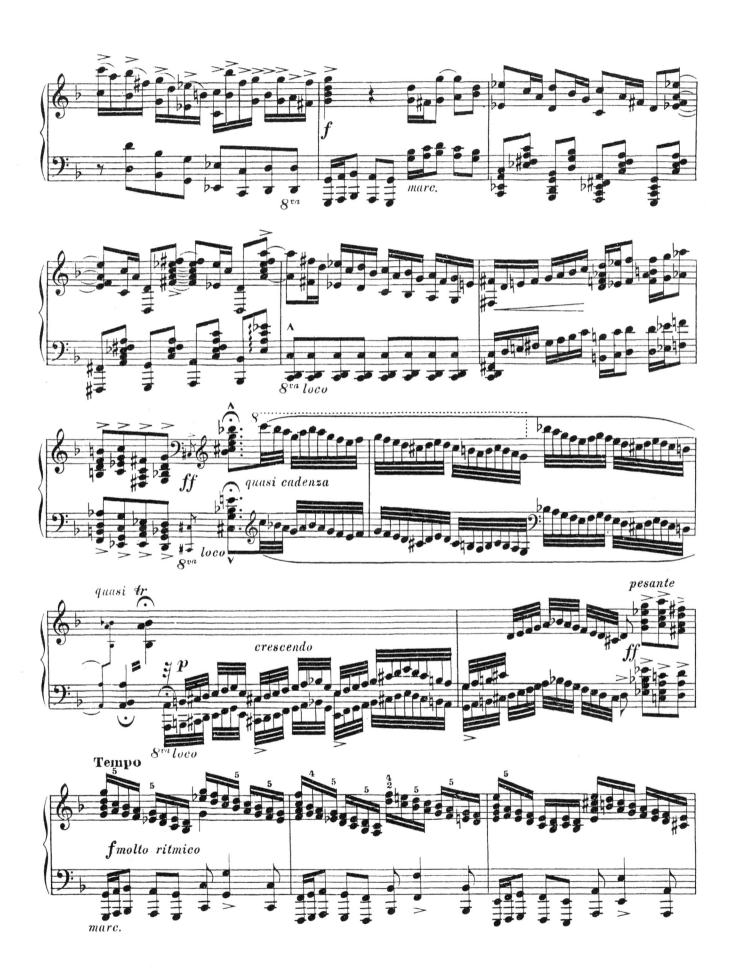

*) The notes shown in brackets, are for small hands.

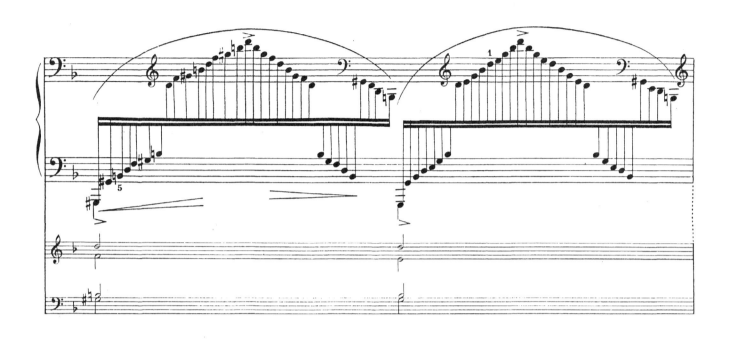
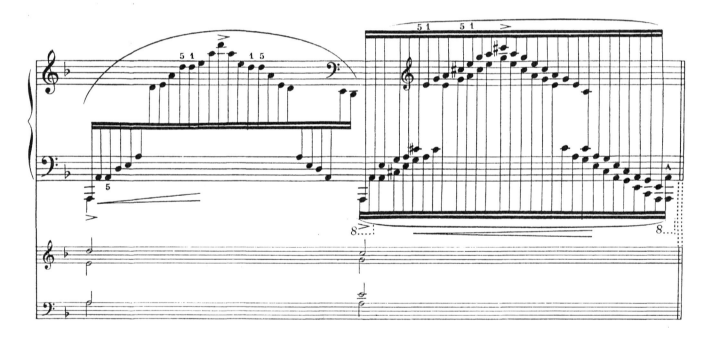